You were a part of me

Sofia J. Ross

Poems:

Foreword

Dear reader,

You are holding a book that is much more than a simple collection of poems and quotes. These pages contain the strength, vulnerability, and hope of a young girl who has experienced the deepest pain and has chosen to transform it into a song of rebirth. This book, titled "You Who Were a Part of Me," is a gift that the author wanted to share with you, hoping that it may heal your wounds and reignite your faith in love.

The author has faced the darkness of disappointment and loss with courage and determination. She has traversed the abyss of betrayed love and found her way towards the light. She has decided to gather her pain, her hopes, and her tears into words that reach straight to the heart. And so, page after page, she weaves a tapestry of poetry that draws from her lived experience, diving into the depths of her soul.

These poems are like delicate threads that intertwine with your own story, your emotions, and your inner struggles. As you read, you will feel the warmth of the author taking your hand and accompanying you on her journey of healing. You can immerse yourself in her disarming sincerity and discover that you are not alone, that the pain you have experienced is shared by many other souls.

But this book does not stop at pain. It is a hymn to hope, rebirth, and the possibility of believing in love again. The author, with her empathetic and authentic voice, urges you to look beyond the scars, to find beauty in vulnerability, and to emerge like a butterfly with wings once again strong and radiant.

Hold this book in your hands as a precious gift, as a companion that supports you along the path to healing. Let the author's words resonate deep within your being and guide you towards a new positive light. May her courage and compassion inspire you to rise again, to believe in love once more, and to discover the wonder of a heart that opens itself to the possibility of loving again.

With affection and hope,

Sofia J. Ross

What could have been but never was.

I wish I could have loved you,
shaped these hidden emotions,
set them free like butterflies in the wind,
but life took us on different paths,
and all that remains
is a bittersweet dream
of what could have been
and never was.

Know that pain will only leave
when it has finished
teaching you its lesson.

If...

If only I had been more present,
perhaps I could have nourished our love
with every small gesture,
I could have felt the warmth of your words,
I could have whispered promises in your ear,
that would have made our bond stronger.

But now,
all I'm left with is regret
for that lost time,
and the hope for a future
where my presence
can still matter to you.

*Abandonment is like a silent shadow
that swallows promises and extinguishes hopes,
leaving the heart in a winter's cold.*

I wish...

I wish to be the bandage that closes every wound,
the balm that soothes every pain,
the light that brightens your darkest moments,
because loving you means
desiring to see happiness
reflected in your eyes,
every day,
every moment.

You were a part of me

Time doesn't fix things,
it helps you understand them.
You have to take care of fixing them yourself.

The wings of freedom.

Letting you go was like releasing
a bird I had nurtured
with love and dedication;
watching it fly away
broke my heart,
but I knew that its freedom
was more important
than my loneliness.

You were a part of me

I spent an entire afternoon
on the couch, staring at the ceiling,
and I think all I did
was think about you.

I'll be with you.

I'll send you a kiss on the wind,
entrusting it to its gentle caresses.
In the whisper of the air,
it will carry my love to you.
Even if you don't see me,
you'll know that I'll be there,
always by your side.

You were a part of me

I am tired
of always moving t
owards someone
who remains motionless.

The cure.

Don't settle for crumbs of affection,
Seek the happiness you deserve, true respect.
Unhappiness is when you deprive yourself of what you
deserve,
Take care of yourself, be true to your dignity.

It's strange how the value of someone's presence becomes evident only when faced with their absence.

Don't settle.

Don't settle for diluted love,
that doesn't ignite the flame in your enamored heart.
Wait with patience, trust, and hope,
for a love that fills you with joy and abundance.

Happiness shines in sincere waiting,
for a love that gives you the light you long for.
Don't fear solitude, don't accept it,
wait for true love that shines like a star.

Unhappiness lies in accepting just anyone to avoid loneliness, but finding true happiness requires the courage to wait for genuine love rather than settling for compromise.

Don't throw yourself away.

Direct your steps towards those who move towards you.
A shared journey doesn't require words.

The rhythm of reciprocity
is the melody that guides the path,
a silent counterpoint to every step.

Only to these dedicate your journey,
until your last breath.

*There will come a time when
those who treated you poorly
will regret it.
But it will be too late for them.*

It's too late now.

Sometimes, we're so busy
walking the paths of others
that we forget our own journey.

And then comes a moment,
a moment suspended between dusk and dawn,
a moment of piercing silence,
when we realize we are lost.

And sometimes, it's too late.
Too late to turn back,
too late to correct the mistakes.

But in that bitter awareness,
there is also a possibility.

The possibility of finding oneself,
of learning from one's mistakes,
of rising from the ashes.

Because it's only when we get lost
that we can truly find ourselves.

Put yourself first once in a while.
It's not selfishness, it's necessary!

I would like...

I would like to do with you what the sun does with the
sea,
awaken the wave, embrace the horizon,
set free the song of the wind.
Dance with you in the time of light,
just as the sun dances upon the sea at twilight.

I would like to be the sun that shines upon your face,
the warmth that melts away your winters,
and the light that reveals your depth.

I would like to do with you what the sun does with the
sea,
renew, shine, awaken.

You were a part of me

Physical attractions are common,
mental connections are rare.

What is love?

Love is an invitation,
extended with tenderness,
not just to the form,
but to the essence.

Not a call
for a embrace of sheets,
but an offering
to share life together.

*You are too valuable
to be the occasional
of someone else.*

Abandonment.

Abandonment moves like a silent shadow,
swallowing promises, extinguishing hopes.
It leaves the heart in a cold solitude,
a winter landscape without any shelter.

But the shadow passes, the heart perseveres,
and, with time, even loneliness can bloom,
revealing, in its silent womb,
a new beginning after the end.

You were a part of me

*If no one is thinking about you,
think about yourself!*

The shadow of your memory.

Your love was like the dawn,
it illuminated me from the darkness,
but like the brightest sun,
it vanished too soon,
leaving me in the shadow of your memory.

Those who did not want when they could,
will not be able to when they want.
Best regards,
Opportunity and Time.

The obstacles of the heart.

The obstacles of the heart
are like invisible walls,
they may seem insurmountable,
but each of them hides a precious lesson.

They teach us to fight,
to persevere,
to respect and love even more,
until, finally,
we find the key to overcome them.

You were a part of me

Actions matter,
not just words.

Since you've been gone.

The days have grown longer
since you went away.
Each sunrise carries the echo of your awakening,
each sunset the shadow of your departure.

There is a silence in which I search for you,
a stillness where I wait for you.
Time has stood still since you went away,
yet it continues to flow,
carrying memories along,
leaving behind unspoken desires.

Since you went away,
you are everywhere and nowhere.

An endless goodbye,
a promise of memories,
a whisper of love in the air I breathe.

There are 8 billion people in the world.
8 billion souls.
And sometimes... you only need one.

One among many...

I thought I was the only one,
the lone star in your night sky.
But your eyes wandered,
seeking other lights,
exploring different horizons.

And in that wandering, I realized:
I was just one among many,
a fleeting reflection
in your infinite universe.

*Nothing is more powerful than
a heart that regains its smile.*

The essential.

You wander through distant lands,
following the sirens' song,
in search of an escape,
a refuge,
a way to forget.

But no matter what you do,
no matter where you go,
you cannot run away from yourself,
you cannot hide in silence.

You are not a drifting leaf,
you are not a lost echo,
you are the wind,
you are the voice,
you are the untamed essence.

Don't try to escape,
don't try to hide.

Embrace yourself,
embrace your light,
be yourself in every moment.

Don't be afraid of losing people.
Be afraid of losing yourself
while trying to please everyone.

Find me.

If you take too long to find me, persevere.
If you can't find me anywhere,
seek elsewhere, for there you will find me,
waiting for you, with open arms.

And if you can't find me, in every corner,
look within yourself, for there I reside.

In the beat of your heart, in the echo of your thoughts,
I am present, inseparably bound to you.

We are all searching for something,
and it often happens that when we find it,
we desire something else.

The flame.

Follow the flame that burns within,
even when everything seems impossible.
Love is the lighthouse that guides the way,
even when the world seems upside down.

I hope you can always see people
exactly for who they are,
and not for who you imagine them to be.

True wealth.

Love does not seek riches or material possessions,
it feeds only on itself, without trivial interests.
It neither appropriates nor allows itself to be possessed,
for love is complete, it needs nothing.

So let love be your guide,
free your heart, embrace its pure light.
Because love, in being what it is,
is the greatest wealth you will ever possess.

*It is not him who keeps hurting you,
but it is you who still give him
the chance to change your mood.*

Without words.

Amidst the noise of the crowd,
in the depths of our being,
we find ourselves,
happy to be together,
speaking through glances,
without the need for words.

In the clamor of the outside world,
we discover an oasis of tranquility,
where love is expressed without words,
in every glance, every smile, every caress.

*Unfortunately, we are often inclined
to judge others.
But remember, things
are not seen as they are,
but as you are.*

My refuge.

You, like the sea,
an endless dance of emotions.
Waves caressing the sand,
storms awakening the soul.

You, calm like a lagoon,
majestic like a hurricane wave.
Your embrace envelops every shore,
bestowing peace and mystery.

In your arms, I find solace,
the comfort I yearn for.
You are the place where I can be myself,
my refuge.

I have lived a full life,
I have traveled all the roads,
and the most important thing
is that I did it my way.

Black hole.

You are a black hole, dark and endless,
Dragging souls into the deepest abyss.
But I have risen, I have moved away from you,
You will no longer be a jailer, for I have found my free-
dom.

Your dark nature, you refuse to acknowledge,
Spreading deceit, causing endless pain.
But I have uncovered the truth, I won't let myself be
swallowed,
I have set myself free, you cannot betray my essence.

You were a part of me

*No matter how hard you try,
you cannot run away from yourself.*

Pieces of me.

The wrong people have a role to play,
they are enchanting stones along the way.
They make me feel the torment of their absence,
but teach me the strength of resilience.

Thus, as the pain merges into the wind,
I discover I'm not alone in my torment.
The pieces of me I've left behind,
are a call to genuine change, defined.

So I smile at the wrong people I've known,
for they have shown my hidden truth, sown.
And as the pain slowly fades away,
I rise stronger, more alive in the present day.

The only thing you can change in others
is your attitude towards them.

I have decided.

I no longer want to wait,
I want to seize the moment,
I want to dance with time,
and live without fear.

I no longer want to wait,
opportunities pass by swiftly,
and I want to seize them all,
before they vanish.

I no longer want to wait,
life is a moving masterpiece,
and I want to be the artist,
painting it without regret.

I no longer want to wait,
because life is here and now,
and in my heart resonates,
the urgency to live without fear.

The hardest thing
is learning
to be alone
again.

I will be there.

I'm here for you, to listen,
when the weight of pain feels overwhelming.
Yes, I understand the weariness you feel,
when the heart is exhausted and the smile fades.

Words may seem empty,
but I want you to know you're not alone.
Be kind to yourself, give yourself time,
to heal, to breathe, to let go.

Explore new paths, one small step at a time,
seeking passions and sources of joy.
Find moments of gratitude in the everyday,
discover the essence of life that still awaits you.

Be kind to yourself, repeat these words,
that everything shall pass.
And remember, even in the darkest night,
the dawn will rise, bringing new hope.

You were a part of me

Allow yourself to feel
all your emotions
without labeling them
in any way.

Navigating.

In the vast ocean of doubts, I sail,
among uncertain waves that dance in time.
But with confidence, I rise like a pristine sail,
discovering my true self without fear.
I find my worth in the depths of the soul,
where an eternal and refined light resides.
I am a sparkling lighthouse, guiding my destiny,
sailing in the ocean of life with a divine smile.

*It is only when you let go
of all the things you hold onto
that don't belong to you,
that you can find your way again.*

Rising again.

In a kaleidoscope of changes, an awakening occurs,
a fiery essence rising from the ashes, undisturbed.
No fear, no frenzy to tame,
the fire within her burns, free to dance its flame.

Old chains break, no regrets to hold,
a bold metamorphosis, boundless and bold.
Past wounds transform into newfound strength,
as she embraces life with fervor and length.

No challenge can extinguish her inner blaze,
for now within her dwells an eternal, superior haze.
Thus, in transformation, she breaks free from the chains,
embracing the authenticity of her newfound reign.

*Have you ever said "goodbye" to someone
and deep down inside, hoped that they would fight
to not let you go?*

Learning to love myself.

There are days when learning to love myself
feels like the boldest adventure I have ever embarked
upon.
A journey within me, through the labyrinth of self-
esteem,
exploring the depths of my most intimate being.

It's a wild feeling, like a rushing torrent,
overwhelming every doubt and fear,
uncovering hidden beauty, precious worth,
residing within me, a treasure to explore.

It's not an easy, nor a linear path,
but an odyssey of discovery and understanding.
Through challenges and moments of vulnerability,
I learn to love myself, to embrace my true essence.

*I made a promise to myself
that I will not go to war with myself
for anyone else, ever again.
This time, I choose me.*

Metamorphosis.

Growing entails transformation,
each flower follows its own rhythm,
not all bloom at the same moment,
but each unleashes its charm in due time.

Some may bloom early, with ardor,
while others take longer to blossom.
Their divergent paths don't signify failure,
but bear witness to the uniqueness of each blooming
flower.

We bloom like flowers, each in our own time,
filling the world with distinct colors and scents.
And as we change form, we discover the truth,
that growth is a wondrous process,
endless and ageless.

You were a part of me

When everything was falling apart,
who were the people that stood by you?

The best weapon.

How many more times will you allow
their weapons to push you to react?
Strength resides within you,
don't let their game hurt you.

Be like the calm and deep ocean,
that remains steadfast despite the waves.
Refuse to succumb to provocation,
and instead choose your true intention.

Do not let their weapons
be a reason to lose your composure.
In your serenity, you will find your strength,
and your "non" response will be your weapon.

You were a part of me

*And I have left pieces of myself
inside the wrong people.*

Like a butterfly.

Like butterflies emerging from their cocoons,
life unfolds in a continuous flow.
There is no obstacle that can stop it,
it always finds a way to carry on.

Butterflies grow their wings with grace,
life expands with courage and trust.
They teach us that transformation is within us,
that evolution is a constant in our existence.

Just as butterflies dance in the air,
life finds a way to take flight.
Through the changes and challenges it faces,
it opens up to new possibilities, to a bright future.

Believe that sooner or later you will have a big laugh,
because remember,
when you no longer care,
everyone comes back.

Towards Spring.

Move forward with confidence towards a new beginning,
as if everything that came before was just a dream,
a long winter now fading away in time.

Advance with steady and hopeful steps,
towards the expanding horizon before you.
What has been is just a chapter of your story,
now is the time to write the future you envision.

Embrace the new beginning with fervor,
as if each day were a promise of rebirth.
Let the past be but a sweet melody,
as you dance towards the enchantment of an infinite
spring.

*Love yourself so much
that you no longer allow anyone
to make you feel wrong.*

The wildflower.

They forget that I am a wildflower,
planted in every place
where they thought
I would never grow.

Self-love is not external validation,
but everything that quietly blossoms within you.

The decision.

You live in anticipation of a heart that beats for you,
at the mercy of others' promises of love.

Will you continue to let yourself be chosen,
to be the rose among a thousand in the garden,
or will you finally open your heart
to decide who deserves your love?

You were a part of me

I am still diligently trying
to find my worth,
in a field full of roses,
I am learning how to handle the thorns.

Survivor.

Pain has made you a survivor,
but it is strength that propels you forward.
In the depths of your soul,
you find the resolve to never give up.

And so, you continue to march towards the future,
guided by the burning flame within you.
Pain has made you a survivor,
but it is your strength that will make you victorious fore-
ver.

A new transformation is taking place,
and she has no intention
of taming the fire
that is erupting from the ashes.

Actions don't lie.

Words, captivating and persuasive,
sometimes get lost in their flow,
while gestures, simple and concrete,
conquer the world without deceit.

Words can deceive and lie,
be traps of sweetness or harshness,
but actions, voiceless, can't betray,
and with their truth often surprise human nature.

How many more times will you allow their weapons
to be the reason for your reaction?

If you return.

No resentment, but the memory lingers,
the pain endured has left a trace.
I don't forget the wounds and tears,
those experiences that have marked my soul.

When you return and find me absent,
perhaps you will understand what you've lost.
Regret may creep in,
as you realize the cost of your actions.

You were a part of me

I imagine you like the sea in Paris,
an enchanted utopia.

Your words no longer hurt.

Your words may hurt, it's true,
but I am no longer your victim.
Now, in the shadow of pain,
I awaken like a flower blooming in the heart.

You will no longer be the architect of my destiny,
your words will never chain me again.
I rise above the hurt you have sown,
and transform into Love.

The Love that you will never find again.

Like butterflies developing their wings,
life always finds a way to move forward.

No regrets.

Do not let regret hinder your stride,
life is a constantly evolving flow.
With courage and determination, overcome the impasse,
and explore the opportunities that await your vision.

Among all the heartbreaks I have experienced,
the one that hurt me the most
was not loving myself.

Be authentic.

Don't succumb to judgment or others' expectations,
free your mind from limiting patterns.
Because you are worthy of love, joy, and happiness,
be true to yourself, to your authenticity.

If you choose not to decide,
you have already made a choice.

The choiche.

The choice is yours alone, don't listen to others' voices,
live according to your values, following your heart.
Don't settle for a life that doesn't reflect who you are,
free yourself from deceit and fear.

Listen to that voice inside you that guides you towards happiness,
don't fear disappointing those who don't understand.
Follow your path, even if it's complicated and challenging,
because only you know your true essence and your destiny.

Saying goodbye hurts, it always will,
but before the pain took root,
love had already blossomed here.

The beautiful things.

The beautiful things in life
are not material objects,
but experiences,
emotions, and connections
that enrich us
and make us feel alive.

The most precious things in life
cannot be owned
or purchased,
but they are intangible
and reside within the heart.

*Sometimes, you have to forget
what you feel
and remember
what you deserve.*

The difference.

The difference is made by those who,
after finding you,
continue to seek you,
to want you by their side.

*When you truly desire something,
the entire universe conspires
to help you achieve it.*

Everything is necessary.

No one enters your life in vain:
either they are a test,
an opportunity for growth,
to learn how to heal,
or they are a gift,
an opportunity to love and rejoice.

While words compete,
gestures cross the finish line.

Truly listening.

I enjoyed truly listening to you.
I'm not talking about words.
I enjoyed listening to your gaze,
your gestures,
your smiles,
your soul,
your heart.

And now,
when they drift away,
you no longer chase them,
because you have understood
your true worth.

The rebirth.

From the shadow of lost love,
a radiant light is born,
a rebirth unfolding,
after the storm I have endured.

The shed tears have cleansed the soul,
freeing the burden of the past,
and in the void left by wounded love,
I found the strength to start anew.

Every fragment of my broken heart,
unites in a mosaic of hope,
and from the ruins of ancient love,
rises my new existence.

I grant myself the freedom to let go,
the chains that held me captive,
I walk towards the horizon,
with determined step and open heart,
knowing that in the flow of life,
rebirth is a gift bestowed upon me.

Everything passes when you let go,
everything arrives when it's the right time,
everything heals when you accept it.